**Digital Guerrilla: Low-Cost Tactics to Win Customers Online**

Copyright © 2024 Reginaldo Osnildo

All rights reserved.

PRESENTATION

DIGITAL GUERRILLA MARKETING

UNDERSTANDING THE TARGET AUDIENCE ON DIGITAL

CREATIVITY OVER BUDGET

THE POWER OF SOCIAL MEDIA

GUERRILLA CONTENT MARKETING

TACTICAL SEO

HACKING EMAIL MARKETING

VIRALIZATION BY DESIGN

STRATEGIC PARTNERSHIPS AND COLLABORATIONS

VIRTUAL EVENTS AND WEBINARS

GAMIFICATION

LOW-COST INFLUENCE MARKETING

NATIVE ADVERTISING AND SPONSORED CONTENT

USER-GENERATED CONTENT (UGC)

DIGITAL FLASH MOBS

CHALLENGES AND COMPETITIONS

EMOTIONAL STORYTELLING

DIGITAL AMBUSH MARKETING

STRATEGIC USE OF PODCASTS

CREATIVE REMARKETING

GUERRILLA TACTICS FOR LOCAL SEO

ANALYSIS AND RAPID ADAPTATION

SMART AUTOMATION

LOW-COST LEAD GENERATION

GUERRILLA ACTION PLAN

REGINALDO OSNILDO

# PRESENTATION

Welcome to the universe where creativity and innovation know no limits, where every challenge is an opportunity in disguise and the conventional gives way to the extraordinary. This is not just another book about digital marketing; is an invitation to embark on a transformative journey with "**Digital Guerrilla: Low-Cost Tactics to Win Customers Online**".

You are about to dive into a world where budget does not define success, but rather the ability to think differently and act boldly. With an unwavering focus on creativity, innovation and unconventional strategies, this book is your ally to stand out in saturated markets and create a striking and effective online presence. Here, every page turn is a step forward on your journey to attract and retain customers on limited budgets, giving you the tools to turn obstacles into stepping stones to success.

In this compendium, you will not only find theories and concepts. You will find a fusion of experience, insight and practice, meticulously adapted for today. Through my lens, I have synthesized and updated the principles of guerrilla marketing for the digital environment, ensuring that each strategy and tactic presented is not only relevant, but immediately applicable to your business.

The structure of this book has been carefully designed to guide you, step by step, through the vast field of digital guerrilla marketing. From understanding your target audience to running viral campaigns and establishing strategic partnerships, each chapter builds on itself, while inviting you to delve even deeper into the next. And whenever I refer to you, know that it is a personal invitation to actively participate in this journey of growth and innovation.

As you turn each page, you will find not just a guide, but a partner on your digital journey. And at the end of this adventure, you will not only have acquired in-depth knowledge about how to apply guerrilla marketing tactics in the digital environment, but you will also have developed the ability to see beyond the obvious, use creativity to overcome limitations and, most importantly, create authentic and lasting connections with your customers.

Are you ready to turn the game in your favor? Are you ready to do more with less, leveraging the power of digital guerrilla marketing to create an unforgettable online presence? So, welcome. Your journey starts now. And remember: the next chapter awaits you with fundamental insights into **DIGITAL GUERRILLA MARKETING** , the cornerstone of this universe. Let's uncover together how this approach can revolutionize your marketing strategy, paving the way for success in an increasingly competitive digital world.

Yours sincerely

Reginaldo Osnildo

# DIGITAL GUERRILLA MARKETING

In a world where attention has become the most valuable currency, digital guerrilla marketing emerges not just as a strategy, but as a necessity for those who want to stand out without necessarily having large budgets. In this chapter, you will understand what digital guerrilla marketing is, its roots, its evolution and, most importantly, how this approach can transform your marketing strategy, making it more effective, memorable and capable of achieving impressive results with limited resources. .

WHAT IS DIGITAL GUERRILLA MARKETING?

Originating from guerrilla tactics used in conflicts, where small groups used unconventional strategies to combat larger and more equipped adversaries, guerrilla marketing adapts this philosophy to the commercial context. In the digital environment, this means using creativity, surprise and innovation to generate significant impact, promoting your brand, products or services.

You, as an entrepreneur or marketer, may be asking yourself, "Is this really for me?" The answer is a resounding yes. Whatever the size of your business or the nature of your market, digital guerrilla marketing offers a unique opportunity to connect with your audience in a deep and meaningful way.

FUNDAMENTALS OF DIGITAL GUERRILLA MARKETING

To successfully embark on this journey, it is essential to understand the three fundamental pillars of digital guerrilla marketing:

- **Creativity over capital:** The essence of guerrilla marketing is using creativity and innovation to overcome budget limitations. It's not about how much you spend, but how you spend it.

- **Focus on the target audience:** Knowing deeply who you are trying to reach is crucial. Digital guerrilla marketing is hyper- targeted, seeking to create personalized experiences that resonate strongly with your specific audience.

- **Measurement and agility:** The ability to measure the impact of your actions and adapt quickly is vital. This allows for an iterative approach, where you learn from each campaign and continually improve.

## TRANSFORMING YOUR STRATEGY

Adopting digital guerrilla marketing can transform your strategy in several ways:

- **Differentiation in the market:** In saturated markets, offering something unique and memorable can be the key to standing out.

- **Deep engagement:** Guerrilla tactics create emotional connections, turning your audience into brand advocates.

- **Maximizing resources:** By optimizing creativity, you achieve impressive results without exhausting your financial resources.

## PRACTICAL APPLICATION

To start, think about actions that can surprise your audience, offer real value and encourage active participation. This can range from viral campaigns on social media to interactive experiences that challenge conventional expectations. The important thing is that each action reflects the authenticity of your brand and speaks directly to the heart of your audience.

As you progress through this chapter, remember: digital guerrilla marketing is not a rigid set of rules, but an invitation to experiment. It's about writing your own rules, testing the limits of what's possible, and most of all, having fun in the process.

By turning this page, you will not only have a solid understanding of the fundamentals of digital guerrilla marketing, but you will also be prepared to dive into the next chapter where we will explore " **UNDERSTANDING THE TARGET AUDIENCE ON DIGITAL"** . In this chapter, we'll uncover techniques for identifying and deeply understanding your online audience, the cornerstone to any successful marketing strategy. Get ready to learn how to deepen your connection with customers in a way that transcends digital, creating an engaged and loyal community. Here we go?

# UNDERSTANDING THE TARGET AUDIENCE ON DIGITAL

The success of any marketing strategy, especially in the context of digital guerrilla marketing, fundamentally depends on how well you know and understand your target audience. This chapter is dedicated to unveiling methods and techniques for identifying and deeply understanding your online audience, allowing you to create campaigns that not only capture attention but also speak directly to the hearts and minds of your potential customers.

THE IMPORTANCE OF KNOWING YOUR AUDIENCE

In digital guerrilla marketing, knowing your target audience goes beyond simple demographics like age, gender and location. It's about understanding your motivations, desires, fears, preferences and online behaviors. This deep understanding allows you to create messages and campaigns that resonate on a personal level, increasing the effectiveness of your marketing strategies and driving genuine engagement.

TECHNIQUES TO IDENTIFY YOUR TARGET AUDIENCE

- **Data analysis and metrics:** Use analytical tools to study your audience's behavior on your website and social networks. Observe interaction patterns, most visited pages, most engaged content, and peak activity times.

- **Surveys and quizzes:** Direct yet powerful tools to gain insights from your audience. Questions should be strategic, aiming to discover not only who they are, but what they value in products or services like yours.

- **Audience segmentation:** Divide your audience into subgroups with similar characteristics or interests. This allows you to further customize your marketing campaigns to meet the specific needs of each segment.

- **Engagement on social media:** Social media is fertile ground for understanding your audience. Join conversations, observe the discussions taking place around your brand and your industry, and pay attention to the type of content that generates the most engagement.

- **Competitor analysis:** Observing how your target audience interacts with competitors can offer valuable insights into your own strengths and areas of opportunity.

APPLYING KNOWLEDGE ABOUT THE PUBLIC

With an in-depth understanding of your target audience, you are now in a prime position to:

- **Personalize communication:** Tailor your message and approach to speak directly to your audience's interests and needs.

- **Create relevant content:** Develop content that not only attracts attention, but also generates value and connection with your audience.

- **Optimize engagement strategies:** Adjust your marketing tactics to maximize interaction and engagement with your audience.

THE CHALLENGE OF CONNECTING

Connecting with your audience on digital goes beyond simply knowing their demographics or preferences. It's about understanding their stories, their challenges and their aspirations. This is the heart of digital guerrilla marketing: creating an authentic connection that transcends the product or service, building a relationship of trust and loyalty.

As we move into the next chapter, " **CREATIVITY OVER BUDGET** ," you'll see how this deep understanding of your audience is the key to innovating and exceeding big budgets in marketing. We'll explore how to utilize creativity not just as a tool, but as an ethos, ensuring that every campaign, every piece of content, and every interaction not only reaches your audience, but also resonates with them in a meaningful and lasting way. Ready to discover how your brand can achieve more by investing less and thinking more creatively? Let's go ahead.

# CREATIVITY OVER BUDGET

In a world where the volume of marketing messages can be overwhelming, creativity emerges not as a luxury, but as a crucial necessity. This chapter is dedicated to inspiring you to look beyond budget numbers and focus on the power of innovation and creativity to overcome big budgets in marketing. Here, we'll explore how creativity not only levels the playing field but also establishes your brand as a notable force in any market.

## THE ART OF DOING MORE WITH LESS

The true beauty of creativity in marketing lies in its ability to do more with less. Instead of competing with massive advertising budgets, creativity allows you to explore new ways to engage and delight your audience, creating memorable experiences that promote brand loyalty and social sharing.

## CREATIVE STRATEGIES TO MAXIMIZE IMPACT

- **Stories that resonate:** Telling stories is an art. Genuine, engaging stories can create an emotional connection with your audience, making your brand more relatable and memorable.

- **Unique experiences:** Think outside the box to create unforgettable experiences for your audience. This can range from an online interactive campaign to a digitally broadcast live event that defies expectations.

- **Impactful visual content:** In a saturated digital environment, visual content — whether through videos, infographics or creative images — can capture your audience's attention quickly and effectively.

- **Strategic partnerships:** Collaborating with other brands, influencers or communities can broaden your reach and add a new dimension to your marketing strategy.

- **Use of alternative platforms:** Don't limit yourself to large social media platforms. Exploring emerging niches and platforms can offer unique opportunities to connect with your audience in innovative ways.

## OVERCOMING THE BUDGET CHALLENGE WITH CREATIVITY

The key to overcoming budget limitations is to see every challenge as an opportunity to innovate. Ask yourself, "How can we do this differently?" This simple question can open up a world of possibilities, encouraging you and your team to think more creatively and strategically.

## MEASURING CREATIVITY SUCCESS

Assessing the impact of your creative strategies is essential. Use specific metrics like engagement, reach, conversion, and brand sentiment to measure success and iterate based on performance. Remember, success in digital guerrilla marketing is not always measured in numbers, but in the impact and connection you create with your audience.

## TOWARDS CONTINUOUS INNOVATION

As you move forward on this digital guerrilla marketing journey, remember that creativity is a renewable resource. Every challenge, every audience feedback and every campaign outcome offers a new opportunity to innovate and improve.

As we prepare to explore the next chapter, " **THE POWER OF SOCIAL MEDIA** ," keep an open mind about how you can use these platforms in unconventional ways to engage and engage your audience. Let's dive into strategies that utilize the full potential of social media, turning every post, every tweet and every share into an opportunity to highlight your brand in a creative and impactful way. Are you ready to discover how social media creativity can amplify your message and captivate your audience? Onward then.

# THE POWER OF SOCIAL MEDIA

Social media has transformed the way we connect, communicate and even do business. In this chapter, we'll explore how you can use social media platforms in unconventional ways to engage and attract your audience, capitalizing on the power of these tools to create a striking and effective online presence.

UNDERSTANDING THE POTENTIAL OF SOCIAL MEDIA

Social networks are more than just channels to promote your product or service; they are vibrant spaces for interaction, sharing and community building. Each platform offers unique features and distinct opportunities to connect with your audience in ways that go beyond the traditional.

UNCONVENTIONAL STRATEGIES TO ENGAGE AND ATTRACT

- **Cross-platform storytelling:** Tell a story that unfolds across multiple platforms, creating an immersive experience for your audience. Each piece of the puzzle across different networks contributes to a larger narrative, encouraging audiences to follow your brand across multiple channels.

- **Interactive engagement campaigns:** Use polls, quizzes, and challenges to encourage direct interaction. These activities not only increase engagement but also provide valuable insights into your audience's preferences and behaviors.

- **Partnerships with micro influencers:** Collaborate with influencers who have a genuine connection with your niche market. They can amplify your message in an authentic way, reaching audiences that might not be accessible through conventional channels.

- **Events and live streams:** Harness the power of live content to create moments of real connection with your audience. Q&A sessions, product launches and behind-the-scenes are effective ways to generate anticipation and engagement.

- **User Generated Content (UGC):** Encourage your audience

to create and share content related to your brand. This not only increases the authenticity of your online presence, but also strengthens the relationship between your brand and your followers.

## MAXIMIZING IMPACT WITH CREATIVITY

The key element to standing out on social media is creativity. In a sea of content, the ideas that break the mold, surprise and delight are the ones that truly capture attention and cultivate a loyal following. Whether through an innovative format, an impactful campaign or simply a unique approach to storytelling, creativity is your greatest ally on social media.

## MEASURING SUCCESS

Social media success can be measured in a number of ways, including engagement, follower growth, traffic driven to your website, and conversions. Platform-specific analytical tools can help you track these metrics and evaluate the performance of your strategies.

As we move into the next chapter, "**GUERRILLA CONTENT MARKETING**," it's crucial to remember that content is the heart of any digital marketing strategy, especially on social media. We'll explore how to create content that not only grabs attention, but also generates buzz and drives action. Ready to dive even deeper into the strategies that will make your brand resonate on an emotional level with your audience? Let's discover together how to transform your ideas into powerful and memorable content.

# GUERRILLA CONTENT MARKETING

In a digital world saturated with messages and advertisements, making your voice heard requires not only creativity, but also a bold, strategic approach. Guerrilla content marketing represents this boldness, emphasizing the creation of content that not only captures attention but also engages audiences in a meaningful way, encouraging sharing and interaction. In this chapter, we'll explore how you can develop and implement content marketing strategies that highlight your brand, generate buzz, and foster an authentic connection with your audience.

## THE ESSENCE OF GUERRILLA CONTENT MARKETING

Guerrilla content marketing goes beyond the traditional, focusing on innovative ideas and executions that capture the public's imagination. It's about being memorable, shareable and, above all, impactful. To do this, your content must:

- **Provoke thought:** Encourage your audience to think differently about a topic, problem or solution.

- **Generate emotion:** Content that evokes emotion – be it joy, surprise or even shock – is more likely to be shared.

- **Encourage action:** Create content that motivates your audience to take action, whether it's sharing, commenting or participating in a discussion.

## STRATEGIES FOR CREATING CONTENT THAT GENERATES BUZZ

- **Tell unique stories:** Stories that resonate on a personal level or that highlight unusual experiences tend to capture attention and encourage sharing.

- **Go for the look:** Visually appealing content, such as infographics, short videos and personalized memes, can significantly increase the engagement and visibility of your content.

- **Create interactive campaigns:** Challenges, quizzes and games not only engage your audience, but can also spread quickly, expanding the reach of your content.

- **Use data creatively:** Presenting data and statistics through visual narratives or stories can transform complex information into interesting and accessible content.

- **Promote user participation:** Encouraging user-generated content not only increases engagement but also provides authentic perspectives on your brand.

OVERCOMING CHALLENGES WITH INNOVATION

Guerrilla content marketing requires a mindset of constant experimentation and a willingness to take risks. Don't be afraid to test new ideas or formats. Analyzing the results of these experiments will provide valuable insights that you can use to further refine your strategies.

MEASURING THE IMPACT OF YOUR CONTENT

Evaluating the success of guerrilla content marketing involves monitoring engagement metrics such as views, shares, comments, and the expansion of content reach. Analytical tools and direct audience feedback are crucial to understanding what resonates with your audience and adjusting your strategies as needed.

As we move into the next chapter, " **TACTICAL SEO** ," it's important to recognize that content marketing and search engine optimization (SEO) go hand in hand. Engaging and creative content not only attracts your audience's attention, but can also significantly improve your online visibility when optimized correctly for SEO. In the next chapter, we will explore search optimization strategies that can be applied without requiring large investments, ensuring that your guerrilla content is found by the right audience at the right time. Are you ready to take your content strategy to the next level? Let's go.

# TACTICAL SEO

In the war for online attention, search engine optimization (SEO) is your strategic positioning strategy. No matter how innovative or engaging your content is, if it isn't found by your target audience, it won't fulfill its purpose. This chapter is dedicated to exploring tactical SEO strategies that don't break the bank, allowing your content to not only be found but also stand out in a competitive digital environment.

TACTICAL SEO FUNDAMENTALS

Before we dive into strategies, it's crucial to understand that tactical SEO is about being smart and strategic with your resources. Focuses on optimizations that deliver the highest return on investment, ensuring each effort contributes significantly to your brand's online visibility.

- **Long-tail keyword research:** Focusing on long-tail keywords (more specific, less competitive phrases) can help you reach a more targeted audience and improve your chances of ranking high in search results.

- **On-page optimization:** Ensure that every page on your website is optimized for search engines, including titles, meta descriptions, headings and the natural inclusion of keywords in the content.

- **Quality content:** Content that is useful, informative and answers your target audience's questions is key. Search engines prioritize sites that offer real value to users.

- **User experience (UX):** An easy-to-navigate, fast and mobile-friendly website not only improves the user experience, but is also an important factor for search rankings.

- **Internal link building:** Internal links not only help with site navigation, but they also establish a hierarchy of information, giving search engines a clear idea of the structure of your content.

## ADVANCED STRATEGIES

In addition to the fundamentals, here are some advanced strategies to take your SEO to the next level:

- **Rich snippet and schema markup optimization:** Adjusting your content to appear as a featured snippet can significantly increase visibility and traffic to your website.

- **Optimization for voice search:** With the increased use of voice assistants, optimizing your content for conversational questions can help you capture this growing market segment.

- **Evergreen content:** Invest in content that remains relevant over time. This type of content can continue to attract traffic and generate value for years.

## MEASURING SUCCESS

The success of your SEO strategies can be measured through a variety of metrics, including keyword rankings, organic traffic, page dwell time, and conversion rates. Tools like Google Analytics and Google Search Console are essential for monitoring performance and identifying areas for optimization.

As we move on to the next chapter, " **HACKING EMAIL MARKETING** ," remember that search engine optimization and content marketing are just parts of a broader digital ecosystem. Integrating SEO strategies with email marketing tactics can not only increase the visibility of your content, but also foster deeper, longer-lasting relationships with your audience. Ready to explore how to turn your emails into a powerful engagement tool? Let's go.

# HACKING EMAIL MARKETING

In the vast universe of digital marketing, email remains one of the most powerful and personal tools at a brand's disposal. Despite being one of the oldest forms of digital communication, email marketing offers a unique opportunity to talk directly to your audience. This chapter will guide you through creative techniques for planning and executing email campaigns that not only get opened and read, but also encourage meaningful action.

REINVENTING EMAIL MARKETING

To successfully hack email marketing, you need to go beyond conventional practices. This means:

- **Advanced personalization:** Use your audience data to personalize each message in a meaningful way. This goes beyond simply inserting the recipient's name into the email; it's about segmenting your list and tailoring content to each segment's specific preferences and behaviors.

- **Subjects that capture attention:** The subject of your email is the first impression. It should be thought-provoking, relevant and, whenever possible, personalized. A/B testing email subject lines can reveal what resonates most with your audience.

- **Optimized design and layout:** Visually appealing emails that are easily readable on mobile devices significantly increase engagement rates. Using visual elements, such as images and GIFs , can help make the message more appealing.

- **Valuable content:** Each email must offer value to the recipient, whether through useful information, entertainment or exclusive offers. Think of each email as an opportunity to provide something of value that strengthens the relationship with your audience.

- **Clear calls to action:** Your email should have a clear objective, with a call to action (CTA) that guides the recipient to the next step. Whether it's reading a blog article, taking advantage of a limited offer, or participating in an event, the CTA must be clear and convincing.

## CREATIVE TECHNIQUES FOR EMAIL CAMPAIGNS

- **Automation with a human touch:** Use automation to ensure timely delivery of your emails, but don't forget to add elements that bring a personal, human touch to the communication.

- **Educational email series:** Create email series that educate your audience on topics relevant to your niche. This establishes your brand as an authority and keeps your audience engaged over time.

- **Interactive emails:** Include interactive elements such as polls, quizzes or videos within the email itself. This can increase interactivity and recipient engagement with the content.

- **Test and optimize:** Continuously test different aspects of your email campaigns, such as send times, frequency, design and CTA. Use the insights you collect to optimize future campaigns.

## MEASURING SUCCESS

The success of email marketing campaigns can be measured by metrics such as open, click, conversion and bounce rates. Email marketing tools offer detailed analyzes that help you understand your audience's behavior and the effectiveness of your strategies.

With the foundations of email marketing reinvented, it's time to look ahead. The next chapter, " **VIRALIZATION BY DESIGN** ", will cover how to create content with the potential to go viral by leveraging the techniques discussed so far and integrating them into a cohesive digital marketing approach. Ready to discover how your content can capture the public's imagination and spread like wildfire across the internet? Let's go ahead.

# VIRALIZATION BY DESIGN

The search for viral content is the Holy Grail of digital marketing. Although there is no exact formula to guarantee virality, understanding the principles that make content widely shared can significantly increase your chances of success. This chapter will explore how you can design your content to have the greatest viral potential by integrating digital guerrilla marketing tactics to create campaigns that not only capture attention but also encourage mass sharing.

UNDERSTANDING VIRALITY

Virality is, in essence, a mass sharing phenomenon that occurs when content resonates so strongly with audiences that they feel compelled to share it. Key elements that often contribute to viral success include:

- **Emotion:** Content that evokes strong emotions, whether joy, surprise, outrage or humor, is much more likely to be shared.

- **Value:** Content that is useful, informative or offers a unique perspective provides tangible value to the audience.

- **Storytelling:** Powerful, well-told stories that connect on a personal or cultural level can quickly go viral.

- **Element of surprise:** Content that breaks expectations or offers something unexpected attracts attention and increases the likelihood of sharing.

DESIGNING FOR VIRALITY

- **Know your audience:** Deeply understanding who your target audience is and what they value is key to creating content that resonates and goes viral.

- **Encourage sharing:** Make it easy and engaging to share your content. Including clear calls to action that encourage sharing can make a big difference.

- **Use social triggers:** Incorporating current topics, popular memes or cultural references can help your content get noticed and shared.

- **Create visually appealing content:** Images, videos and graphics not only capture attention, they are also formats that people love to share.

- **Test and adjust:** Use A/B testing to experiment with different approaches and messages. Analyzing the results can reveal what most effectively induces sharing.

## FOLLOWING AND ENJOYING VIRALITY

When content starts to go viral, it's crucial to monitor it closely and seize the moment. Respond quickly to comments and interactions to maintain momentum. Additionally, be prepared to adapt or expand your campaign based on audience response to maximize impact.

## MEASURING SUCCESS

Viral success can be measured by the number of shares, views, comments, and the overall reach of the content. Social analytics tools can provide detailed insights into how content is performing and who is engaging with it.

With an understanding of how to design for virality, the next step is to explore " **STRATEGIC PARTNERSHIPS AND COLLABORATIONS** ." These can be powerful tools to further expand the reach of your content and solidify your brand's presence in the digital space. In the next chapter, we'll discover how to leverage partnerships and collaborations to create even more impactful and memorable campaigns. Are you ready to expand your reach and strengthen your digital guerrilla marketing strategy? Let's move forward.

# STRATEGIC PARTNERSHIPS AND COLLABORATIONS

Unity is strength, especially in the world of digital marketing, where strategic partnerships and collaborations can be the catalyst for reaching new audiences and solidifying your online presence. This chapter will explore how you can identify potential partners, create mutually beneficial collaborations, and use these alliances to broaden your reach and reinforce your brand's authority in the marketplace.

IDENTIFYING POTENTIAL PARTNERS

The first step to a successful partnership is identifying the right partners. Look for companies, influencers, or content creators that share a similar target audience but are not direct competitors. Also consider those whose values and mission align with those of your brand, as this can increase the authenticity and impact of the collaboration.

CREATING MUTUALLY BENEFICIAL COLLABORATIONS

A successful collaboration must offer clear value to both parties involved, as well as their respective audiences. This may include:

- **Co-created campaigns:** Develop marketing or content campaigns that combine the strengths and resources of both brands to create something exciting.

- **Content exchange:** Consider guest blogging or co-creating webinars and podcasts that can benefit both parties' audiences.

- **Shared offers or promotions:** Create exclusive offers or discounts that encourage audiences from both brands to interact and cross-purchase.

- **Joint events:** Organize events, whether virtual or in-person, that bring together communities from both brands to learn, share and connect.

LEVERAGING PARTNERSHIPS TO EXPAND REACH

Once the partnership is established, it is critical to carefully plan how you will promote it to maximize its reach and impact. Use all available channels - social networks, email marketing, blogs, etc. - to publicize the collaboration. Encouraging public sharing and participation through contests or special hashtags can also help increase visibility.

MEASURING PARTNERSHIP SUCCESS

The success of a partnership can be measured through several indicators, including increase in followers, engagement, website traffic, and, of course, sales or conversions. Establish clear success metrics with your partner from the start, and use analytics tools to monitor collaboration performance.

With strategic partnerships and collaborations well planned and implemented, the next chapter, " **VIRTUAL EVENTS AND WEBINARS** ", will dive into how to use online events as a powerful engagement and community-building tool. Ready to explore the potential of virtual events to connect, educate and inspire your audience? Let's go together on this next stage of the digital guerrilla marketing journey.

# VIRTUAL EVENTS AND WEBINARS

Virtual events and webinars have emerged as essential tools in the digital marketing toolbox, offering innovative ways to engage audiences, share knowledge and strengthen the community around your brand. This chapter will guide you on how to plan and execute online events that not only capture your audience's attention, but also foster meaningful connections and promote brand loyalty.

WHY VIRTUAL EVENTS AND WEBINARS?

The accessibility and convenience of online events make them especially attractive to global audiences. They allow:

- **Expanded reach:** Overcoming geographic barriers, reaching a wider audience than would be possible with in-person events.

- **Deep engagement:** Interact directly with your audience, answering questions in real time and adapting content to their needs and interests.

- **Building authority:** Position your brand as a thought leader by sharing valuable knowledge and insights.

- **Cost-efficiency:** Significantly reduce costs associated with holding in-person events, such as space rental, catering and logistics.

PLANNING SUCCESSFUL VIRTUAL EVENTS

- **Define your goals:** Whether educating about a new product, building community or generating leads, having clear goals is crucial to the success of the event.

- **Know your audience:** Understanding who your audience is and what they expect from the event will help shape your content and promotion strategy.

- **Choose the right platform:** Evaluate different virtual event and webinar platforms based on features such as audience capacity, engagement tools, and customization options.

- **Create engaging content:** Develop an agenda with interesting speakers, relevant topics, and interaction opportunities to keep your audience engaged.

- **Promote your event:** Use all available channels – email, social networks, partnerships – to publicize the event and encourage registrations.

MAXIMIZING ENGAGEMENT AND INTERACTION

During the event, promote active interaction through:

- **Live Q&A:** Set aside time for Q&A, allowing the audience to interact directly with the speakers.
- **Polls and Surveys:** Collect real-time audience feedback and opinions to increase engagement.
- **Virtual Networking:** Encourage networking among participants using chat rooms or virtual "table" features.

POST-EVENT: EVALUATION AND CONTINUITY

After the event, it is important:

- **Send Thank You and Feedback Surveys:** Thank attendees for their attendance and solicit feedback to improve future events.

- **Make recorded content available:** Offer access to event content to those who were unable to attend live, extending the value of your event.

- **Analyze results:** Evaluate the success of the event based on the defined objectives, using metrics such as participation rate, engagement during the event and public feedback.

Now that we've explored how virtual events and webinars can be used to engage and build a community around your brand, the next chapter, "**GAMIFICATION**", will dive into how to incorporate gaming elements to further encourage audience engagement and loyalty . Ready to discover how gamification can transform your audience's experience? Let's go ahead.

# GAMIFICATION

Gamification uses game design elements in non-game contexts, seeking to increase audience engagement and motivation through fun and reward. In this chapter, you'll learn how to incorporate gamification into your digital guerrilla marketing strategy to encourage interaction, loyalty, and even conversion with your audience in innovative and memorable ways.

WHY GAMIFICATION?

Gamification capitalizes on two fundamental aspects of human psychology: the need for reward and the desire for competition. By integrating these elements into your marketing strategy, you can:

- **Increase engagement:** Game elements keep users interested and engaged for longer.

- **Encourage specific actions:** Use rewards to motivate your audience to complete desired tasks, such as filling out surveys, sharing content, or making purchases.

- **Promote learning and exploration:** Games can be an effective way to educate your audience about your products or services in a fun and interactive way.

- **Strengthen brand loyalty:** Positive and rewarding experiences can increase user loyalty and brand advocacy.

IMPLEMENTING GAMIFICATION ELEMENTS

- **Point systems:** Offer points for specific actions, such as interacting with content, making purchases or recommending friends. Points can be exchanged for exclusive rewards or benefits.

- **Achievements and badges:** Recognize and reward users' milestones with visible achievements or badges, encouraging them to stay engaged.

- **Leaderboards:** Promote a sense of healthy competition by displaying users' scores or achievements on leaderboards, motivating them to improve their performance.

- **Challenges and missions:** Create tasks or missions that users can complete in exchange for rewards. These activities should be fun and aligned with your marketing campaign goals.

- **Narratives:** Use engaging stories to guide the gamification experience, increasing emotional engagement and connection with the brand.

CONSIDERATIONS WHEN GAMIFYING

- **Align with your marketing goals:** Make sure gamification elements align with your brand's goals and values.

- **Keep it accessible:** The experience should be easy to understand and participate in, ensuring it doesn't exclude users less familiar with gaming.

- **Offer real value:** Rewards and benefits must offer genuine value to encourage participation and promote loyalty.

- **Monitor and adjust:** Collect data on how users interact with gamification elements and be ready to make adjustments based on feedback and performance.

With a solid understanding of how gamification can enrich your digital guerrilla marketing strategy, the next chapter, " **LOW-COST INFLUENCE MARKETING** ", will explore how working with influencers can maximize your brand's impact, even on a limited budget. Are you ready to discover how to combine influence and gamification to create powerful, engaging campaigns? Let's continue our journey.

# LOW-COST INFLUENCE MARKETING

Influencer marketing has become an essential tool in the digital marketing arsenal, allowing brands to reach specific audiences in an authentic and trustworthy way. However, many small businesses and startups believe that working with influencers is expensive and out of reach. This chapter will demystify this notion by exploring how you can implement an effective, low-cost influencer marketing strategy by leveraging the power of micro influencers to broaden your reach and strengthen your connection with your audience.

THE POWER OF MICRO INFLUENCERS

Micro influencers are individuals who have a smaller number of followers (usually between 1,000 and 100,000) on social media platforms, but have a high level of engagement and a strong, personal connection with their audience. They are perceived as more authentic and trustworthy, making their recommendations more influential.

BENEFITS OF LOW-COST INFLUENCE MARKETING

- **Cost-efficiency:** Working with micro influencers generally requires a smaller investment compared to celebrities or large-scale influencers.

- **High engagement:** Micro influencers' audiences tend to be more engaged, which can lead to higher conversion rates.

- **Audience relevance:** Micro influencers often operate in specific niches, allowing you to reach a highly segmented audience relevant to your brand.

HOW TO IMPLEMENT A LOW-COST INFLUENCER MARKETING STRATEGY

- **Identify the right influencers:** Look for influencers who share similar values with your brand and who have an audience aligned with your target audience.

- **Build genuine relationships:** Before proposing a

collaboration, start a genuine relationship with the influencers. Comment on their posts, share their content and show genuine interest in their activities.

- **Personalized proposals:** Make proposals that respect the interests and style of influencers, suggesting partnerships that are mutually beneficial and aligned with your audiences.

- **Focus on co-creation:** Work together with influencers to co-create content. This not only ensures authenticity, but also leverages the influencers' creativity and experience to create something unique.

- **Measure results:** Define clear KPIs (Key Performance Indicators ) for your influencer marketing campaign, including reach, engagement, traffic or conversions, and use analytics tools to track performance.

CHALLENGES AND CONSIDERATIONS

- **Brand alignment:** Ensure that the influencer's message and image are in tune with your brand to maintain coherence and authenticity.

- **Transparency:** Partnership disclosures must be clear and transparent to the public, in accordance with regulatory guidelines.

- **Realistic expectations:** Understand that influencer marketing is just one part of a broader marketing strategy and must be combined with other efforts to maximize impact.

Armed with an understanding of how to implement a low-cost influencer marketing strategy, the next chapter, " **NATIVE ADVERTISING AND SPONSORED CONTENT** ", will explore how you can effectively use sponsored content to promote your brand while maintaining authenticity and providing value to your audience. Ready to dive deeper into integrating influencer marketing with content strategies? Let's go ahead.

# NATIVE ADVERTISING AND SPONSORED CONTENT

Native advertising and sponsored content emerge as powerful solutions for brands that want to promote their products or services in a subtle and integrated way, avoiding the intrusiveness of traditional ads. This chapter explores how you can utilize these strategies to strengthen brand awareness, improve engagement, and ultimately drive conversions while maintaining a high level of authenticity and providing genuine value to your audience.

## UNDERSTANDING NATIVE ADVERTISING AND SPONSORED CONTENT

Native advertising refers to any type of paid content that naturally adapts to the environment in which it is displayed, both in format and function. Sponsored content is a specific form of native advertising, where advertisers pay to have their content displayed within a publisher 's platform , resembling standard editorial content.

## ADVANTAGES OF THE NATIVE APPROACH

- **Lower audience resistance:** Because it blends naturally with organic content, native advertising is less invasive and can reduce audience resistance to ads.

- **Greater engagement:** Relevant, high-quality content tends to engage more readers, resulting in higher click-through rates and better retention.

- **Strengthening brand credibility:** Associating your brand with valuable, informative content can help build trust and establish authority in your industry.

## HOW TO IMPLEMENT EFFECTIVELY

- **Choose publishing partners carefully:** Select platforms that share your target audience and have a reputation for high-quality content that aligns with your brand.

- **Focus on quality and relevance:** Content must provide real value to the audience, whether through useful information, entertainment or solutions to common problems.

- **Maintain transparency:** It is crucial to be transparent about the sponsored nature of content, following regulatory guidelines and maintaining trust with your audience.

MEASURING SUCCESS

The success of your native advertising campaigns and sponsored content can be measured through several metrics, including:

- **Reach and impressions:** The number of people exposed to your content.

- **Engagement:** Measured by clicks, shares, comments and time spent on content.

- **Conversions:** The desired action taken after exposure to content, such as signups, downloads, or purchases.

CHALLENGES AND CONSIDERATIONS

- **Alignment with organic content:** The challenge is to create sponsored content that aligns so well with the platform's organic content that it maintains the public's interest and trust.

- **Balance between promotion and value:** Finding the right balance between promoting your brand and providing useful content is key to the success of native advertising.

With a robust understanding of how to navigate the world of native advertising and sponsored content, the next chapter, " **USER-GENERATED CONTENT (UGC)** ", will explore how you can encourage and leverage user-created content to drive authenticity, engagement, and growth organic. Are you ready to discover the power of user-generated content in your marketing strategy? Let's proceed.

# USER-GENERATED CONTENT (UGC)

User-generated content (UGC) refers to any form of content —whether text, photos, videos, reviews, or comments—created and published by unpaid users or fans. It represents one of the most authentic and powerful forms of engagement, as it reflects people's real experiences with your brand. This chapter explores how to encourage the creation of UGC and how to effectively utilize it to increase your brand's authenticity, improve engagement, and drive conversion.

BENEFITS OF UGC

- **Authenticity:** User-created content is perceived as more genuine than traditional marketing, building trust and credibility with your audience.

- **Engagement:** UGC encourages active community participation, creating a virtuous cycle of interaction and engagement.

- **Diverse content:** Leveraging UGC provides a constant stream of new and varied content, keeping your brand fresh and relevant.

- **Social proof:** Showing how other customers interact with and appreciate your brand can positively influence purchasing decisions.

HOW TO ENCOURAGE UGC

- **Create engagement campaigns:** Launching challenges, contests or campaigns with specific hashtags can motivate your audience to create and share content related to your brand.

- **Make sharing easy:** Offer easy-to-use tools and platforms so users can effortlessly share their experiences.

- **Offer incentives:** Rewards such as discounts, giveaways or recognition on social media can be great motivators for creating UGC.

- **Ask for permission and give credit:** Always ask for permission before using a user's content and give appropriate credit when posting it on your official channels.

## USING UGC IN YOUR MARKETING STRATEGY

- **Integrate UGC into your platform:** Showcase user-generated content on your website, especially on product pages, to add social proof and influence purchasing decisions.

- **Highlight UGC on social media:** Regularly share UGC on your social media to strengthen the community and encourage more users to participate.

- **Use UGC in email marketing campaigns:** Including user reviews and photos in emails can increase open and conversion rates.

- **Create stories with UGC:** Utilize user content to tell stories that resonate with your target audience, showing different ways your product or service positively impacts their lives.

## MEASURING THE IMPACT OF UGC

Measure UGC success by monitoring:

- **Engagement:** Likes, shares, comments and general participation in the campaign.

- **Reach:** The number of people exposed to UGC related to your brand.

- **Conversions:** The impact of UGC on sales, downloads or other desired actions.

Now that you understand the value of UGC and how to incorporate it into your digital guerrilla marketing strategy, the next chapter, " **DIGITAL FLASH MOBS** ," will explore another innovative tactic for capturing your audience's attention and creating memorable moments. Ready to explore how to organize surprise online events that engage and excite your audience? Let's move on to find out.

# DIGITAL FLASH MOBS

Digital flash mobs are surprise online events, planned to happen suddenly on various digital platforms, bringing people together to carry out a specific action in a short period of time. This tactic, inspired by physical flash mobs that brought people together in public places to carry out a coordinated activity, has adapted to the digital environment as a creative way to capture attention and engage the public. In this chapter, we'll explore how to organize digital flash mobs that not only surprise and delight, but also promote your brand in innovative and effective ways.

PLANNING A DIGITAL FLASH MOB

- **Set a clear goal:** Whether it's launching a new product, raising awareness about a cause, or simply engaging the community, having a clear goal is crucial.

- **Choose the platform:** Depending on your target audience and objective, choose the most suitable platform—it could be Twitter, Instagram, TikTok or even a specific forum.

- **Mobilize your community:** Convening a base of loyal participants in advance, without revealing too many details, can ensure that your digital flash mob has the desired impact.

- **Create a unique hashtag:** A unique hashtag not only helps track participation but also expands the reach of your event.

- **Plan content:** Decide what the action will be—it could be posting a specific photo, sharing a private message, or changing profiles simultaneously.

RUNNING FLASH MOB

- **Communicate specific details covertly:** Inform attendees of the date, time and specific actions just before the event to maintain the element of surprise.

- **Synchronize the launch:** Make sure all participants know the exact moment to start, creating an immediate and coordinated impact.

- **Monitor in real time:** Be aware of the execution of the flash mob, interacting with participants and sharing their content to increase engagement.

MAXIMIZING IMPACT

- **Encourage sharing:** In addition to initial participants, encourage sharing of the flash mob by the wider audience to increase reach.

- **Use influencers:** Engage influencers to participate and share the flash mob with their followers, significantly expanding its impact.

- **Analyze and share results:** After the event, compile the best moments and share the results with your community, celebrating collective success and encouraging future participation.

MEASURING SUCCESS

The success of a digital flash mob can be measured by:

- **Engagement:** Evaluate the number of posts, shares, comments and interactions with the event hashtag.

- **Reach:** Monitor how many people were reached by the flash mob actions.

- **Brand impact:** Observe changes in brand perception, website traffic, or conversions that can be attributed to the event.

Understanding the dynamics and potential of digital flash mobs to engage and surprise your audience, the next chapter, " **CHALLENGES AND COMPETITIONS** ", will dive into how to create and manage online challenges and competitions that encourage active participation and promote the brand in a fun and competitive. Ready to explore how to use challenges to capture your audience's imagination and encourage engagement? Let's move forward in this engaging adventure.

# CHALLENGES AND COMPETITIONS

Online challenges and competitions are powerful tools for engaging your audience, generating interesting content and promoting your brand in a fun and interactive way. They encourage active participation, fostering a vibrant and engaged community around your brand. In this chapter, we'll explore how to create, promote, and manage challenges and competitions that not only capture your audience's imagination but also encourage meaningful interaction and social sharing.

PLANNING YOUR CHALLENGE OR COMPETITION

- **Set clear objectives:** Whether it's increasing engagement, expanding your reach, or collecting UGC, having clear objectives will help shape your challenge or competition.

- **Choose an attractive theme:** The theme must be relevant to your brand and interesting to your audience. It could be something aligned with current events, holidays, or popular trends.

- **Establish simple and clear rules:** The rules must be easy to understand and follow, ensuring broad and fair participation.

- **Decide on prizes:** Prizes must be desirable and appropriate to the effort required to participate. They can range from exclusive products to public recognition.

PROMOTING YOUR COMPETITION

- **Use all available channels:** Promote your competition on all social platforms, on your website and through email marketing to ensure maximum visibility.

- **Engage influencers:** Partnerships with influencers can help expand the reach of your competition and encourage participation.

- **Create a unique hashtag:** A unique hashtag not only helps track entries, but also makes it easier to spread the word about the challenge or competition.

## MANAGING THE CHALLENGE OR COMPETITION

- **Monitor participation:** Track registrations and participation using the hashtag and the tools available on the chosen platform.

- **Maintain engagement:** Interact with participants throughout the competition, commenting and sharing their entries to maintain enthusiasm.

- **Be transparent in selecting winners:** Establish a clear and fair process for choosing winners, whether by public voting or a panel of judges.

## MEASURING SUCCESS

The success of challenges and competitions can be assessed by:

- **Participation:** The number of entries received and the diversity of participants.

- **Engagement:** Likes, shares, comments and other forms of interaction generated by the competition.

- **Reach and growth:** The increase in reach and followers as a direct result of competition.

After exploring the dynamics and potential of online challenges and competitions, the next chapter, " **EMOTIONAL STORYTELLING** ", will delve into how you can use powerful storytelling to create deep emotional connections with your audience. Are you ready to discover how impactful stories can not only engage, but also inspire action and loyalty to your brand? Let's move forward on this narrative journey.

# EMOTIONAL STORYTELLING

Emotional storytelling is a powerful tool in marketing, capable of creating deep connections between brands and their audiences. Narratives that touch the heart can inspire action, cultivate loyalty and generate lasting brand memory in the minds of consumers. This chapter explores how you can use emotional storytelling to not only engage your audience, but also drive identification and loyalty to your brand.

THE IMPORTANCE OF EMOTIONAL STORYTELLING

Stories that evoke strong emotions—be they joy, surprise, sadness, or hope—have the power to connect on a much deeper level than any statistic or list of product benefits. They humanize your brand, making it more relatable and memorable.

ELEMENTS OF AN IMPACT STORY

- **Relatable characters:** Create characters that your audience can identify with or aspire to be like. They are the heart of your story.

- **Conflict and resolution:** Every good story has a conflict that needs to be resolved. This conflict creates tension and interest, while resolution provides satisfaction and closure.

- **Narrative arc:** A clear narrative arc, with a beginning, middle and end, guides the audience through the story, keeping them engaged and invested in the outcome.

- **Emotional appeal:** The story must evoke a specific emotion or series of emotions, creating an immersive experience for the audience.

IMPLEMENTING EMOTIONAL STORYTELLING

- **Define your goals:** Before creating your story, define what you want to achieve. This will help direct the tone and message of the narrative.

- **Know your audience:** Understanding who your audience is and what resonates with them is crucial to creating a story that touches them emotionally.

- **Be authentic:** Your stories should reflect your brand's values and mission. Authenticity creates trust and credibility.

- **Use multiple channels:** Take advantage of different channels—social media, blog, email, video—to tell your story, adapting it to the format that best fits each platform.

MEASURING THE IMPACT OF EMOTIONAL STORYTELLING

The impact of emotional storytelling can be measured through:

- **Engagement:** Likes, shares, comments and views can indicate how resonant your story is with the audience.

- **Direct feedback:** Consumer comments and messages can provide valuable insights into how the story emotionally affected your audience.

- **Conversions:** Increase in sales, sign-ups, or any other desired action after exposure to the story can signal your success in motivating action.

With a deep understanding of how emotional storytelling can enrich your brand communication and create lasting bonds with your audience, the next chapter, " **DIGITAL AMBUSH MARKETING** ", will dive into how to associate your brand with events or trends without being the official sponsor, exploring creative tactics to stand out. Ready to embrace the power of storytelling and explore new frontiers in digital marketing? Let's continue our journey.

# DIGITAL AMBUSH MARKETING

Digital ambush marketing is a cunning strategy that involves associating your brand with significant events, trends, or cultural moments without being an official sponsor. This creative approach can capture audience attention and generate conversations around your brand, leveraging the relevance of the moment to stand out in a cost-effective way. In this chapter, we will explore how to implement digital ambush marketing tactics ethically and effectively, ensuring your brand benefits from these opportunities without infringing rights or alienating your audience.

## UNDERSTANDING DIGITAL AMBUSH MARKETING

Digital ambush marketing takes advantage of the visibility and excitement around popular events or trends by creating campaigns or content that in some way relates to the event, but without an official association. The key is to be creative and subtle, finding innovative ways to connect your brand to the moment without implying a formal partnership.

## KEY ELEMENTS FOR SUCCESS

- **Select relevant moments:** Focus on events or trends that naturally align with your brand's values and personality to ensure the authenticity of the connection.

- **Be creative but respectful:** Find original ways to join the conversation without disrespecting event organizers or sponsorship rights.

- **Agility is key:** Timing is everything in ambush marketing. Be quick to seize opportunities as they arise while maintaining relevance and impact.

- **Focus on generating value:** Content or campaigns must add value to the public, whether through entertainment, information or inspiration, instead of just trying to divert attention to your brand.

## IMPLEMENTING AMBUSH MARKETING STRATEGIES

- **Hashtags and social media:** Use relevant hashtags and participate in social media conversations to organically link your brand to the event or trend.

- **Thematic content:** Create content that reflects the event or trend, such as blog posts, videos or infographics, that may interest the audience following the moment.

- **Special promotions:** Launch promotions or special offers that coincide with the event, attracting those interested in the topic to your brand.

- **Strategic partnerships:** Collaborate with influencers or other brands who are not official sponsors, but who are equally interested in capitalizing on the moment.

## NAVIGATING ETHICAL AND LEGAL ISSUES

When executing ambush marketing strategies, it is crucial to consider ethical and legal issues:

- **Avoid confusion:** Make sure your campaign doesn't create a false impression that your brand is an official sponsor or otherwise endorsed by the event.

- **Respect copyrights and trademarks:** Do not use event logos, slogans or any other copyrighted assets in your campaigns.

- **Transparency:** Be transparent with your audience about the unofficial nature of your participation in the event or trend.

With well-planned and executed digital ambush marketing strategies, the next chapter, " **STRATEGIC USE OF PODCASTS** ", will explore how your brand can harness the growing power of podcasts to reach new audiences and deepen the connection with your existing audience. Are you ready to explore the potential of podcasts in your digital marketing strategy? Let's move forward.

# STRATEGIC USE OF PODCASTS

Podcasts have become one of the most consumed media globally, offering a unique platform for brands to share stories, knowledge and connect deeply with an engaged audience. In this chapter, we'll discuss how to strategically use podcasts in your digital marketing strategy, whether creating your own podcast or leveraging existing podcasts, to expand your reach and strengthen your brand's online presence.

THE RISE OF PODCASTS

With the growing number of listeners looking for relevant and engaging content, podcasts offer a direct channel to capture audience attention in a meaningful way. They allow for a more personal connection with listeners, as they are often consumed in an intimate way, through headphones, creating a sense of closeness between the presenter and the audience.

CREATING YOUR OWN PODCAST

- **Define your niche and goals:** Identify a theme that not only resonates with your target audience, but also aligns with your brand's values and goals.

- **Plan content:** Develop an editorial calendar with interesting topics and guests that can add value to your audience.

- **Focus on quality:** Invest in good sound quality and editing to ensure your podcast is enjoyable and professional.

- **Promote your podcast:** Use all available platforms, including social media, your website and partnerships with other podcasts to promote your program.

PARTICIPATING IN EXISTING PODCASTS

- **Identify relevant podcasts:** Search for podcasts that already serve your target audience and whose themes and values are aligned with your brand.

- **Offer genuine value:** When appearing as a guest, focus on offering valuable insights, stories, and content that benefit the podcast audience.

- **Prepare for the interview:** Get to know the podcast audience well and prepare discussion points that are informative, inspiring and that, in a subtle way, highlight your brand.

- **Promote your appearance:** Share your podcast appearance on your own platforms to maximize reach and provide additional content to your followers.

MEASURING SUCCESS

The success of your podcast strategy can be measured through:

- **Audience:** Number of listeners, downloads and subscriptions to your podcast.

- **Engagement:** Comments, ratings and shares of your podcast or episodes in which you participated as a guest.

- **Conversions:** Increase in traffic to your website or in specific conversions, such as newsletter signups or sales, attributable to your podcast strategy.

Now that we've explored the potential of podcasts as a digital marketing tool, the next chapter, " **CREATIVE REMARKETING** ", will cover how to re-engage past visitors to your website and convert them into loyal customers using innovative, personalized messaging. Ready to explore advanced remarketing techniques to maximize the return on your digital marketing investment? Let's move on to find out.

# CREATIVE REMARKETING

Creative remarketing represents a dynamic strategy for re-engaging visitors who have previously interacted with your website or online platform, but who, for whatever reason, did not complete a desired action, such as a purchase. Using personalized and innovative messaging, this approach aims to not only remind these visitors of your brand, but also encourage effective conversion. In this chapter, we'll discuss how to implement creative remarketing tactics that capture your audience's attention and maximize the return on your digital marketing investment.

UNDERSTANDING REMARKETING

Remarketing, or retargeting, uses cookies to track users across the web and display specific ads based on their past online behavior. This technique offers a second chance to convert interested visitors by applying a more targeted and personal approach.

ELEMENTS OF A SUCCESSFUL REMARKETING CAMPAIGN

- **Efficient segmentation:** Divide your audience based on specific behaviors, such as visitors who abandoned their cart, viewed a specific product page, or spent a certain amount of time on the website.

- **Personalized messaging:** Create ads that speak directly to the experiences and interests of these segments, addressing potential objections or offering incentives for conversion.

- **Creativity in design:** Use attractive visual elements and clear messages that stand out and reinforce your brand identity.

- **Offers and incentives:** Include special promotions, discounts or exclusive gifts to motivate people to return to the site and complete the purchase.

INNOVATIVE REMARKETING TACTICS

- **Dynamic ads:** Use ads that automatically adjust to show specific products or services that the visitor viewed, making the ad more relevant and attractive.

- **Ad sequences:** Develop a series of ads that build a narrative or offer additional information over time, maintaining interest and gently nudging the user back toward conversion.

- **Social remarketing:** Leverage social media platforms for remarketing, where you can utilize demographic and interest information for even more precise targeting.

- **Email Remarketing:** For users who have provided their email addresses, personalized email campaigns can be extremely effective, especially when combined with offers or abandoned cart reminders.

MEASURING AND OPTIMIZING REMARKETING

Measure the success of your remarketing campaigns by monitoring:

- **Conversion rates:** The increase in conversions is a clear indicator of the effectiveness of your remarketing campaign.

- **Cost per conversion:** Analyze the cost of each conversion to ensure that remarketing is providing a good return on investment.

- **Engagement:** Metrics such as time on site and pages visited after the click can help assess the level of re-engagement.

Equipped with creative remarketing strategies, the next chapter, " **GUERILLA TACTICS FOR LOCAL SEO** ," will dive into specific techniques for optimizing your online presence in local search, helping you capture the attention of potential customers in your geographic area. Are you ready to explore how to strengthen your local SEO strategy and stand out in your community? Let's continue this journey to maximize your local visibility.

# GUERRILLA TACTICS FOR LOCAL SEO

Local SEO is essential for businesses that want to increase their visibility to customers in their immediate geographic area. By applying guerrilla tactics to local SEO, even businesses with limited budgets can significantly improve their position in local search results, capturing the attention of potential customers when they are most likely to convert. In this chapter, we will explore innovative, low-cost strategies for optimizing your online presence in the local context.

LOCAL SEO FUNDAMENTALS

Local SEO focuses on optimizing your online presence to appear in search results when users make queries specific to your region. This includes optimizing your website and content for local keywords, as well as actively managing your listing on Google My Business and local online directories.

EFFECTIVE LOW-COST STRATEGIES

- **Google My Business Optimization:** Ensure your listing is complete, accurate, and optimized with up-to-date information, high-quality photos, and relevant categories. Encourage customer reviews and respond to all, whether positive or negative.

- **Local keywords in content:** Incorporate local keywords into your website, including titles, meta descriptions, and content. This helps improve your visibility for region-specific search queries.

- **Localized content creation:** Produce content that resonates with your local audience, such as city guides, blog posts about local events, or case studies from customers in the region. This not only improves SEO but also strengthens community connection.

- **Local partnerships and link building:** Collaborate with other local businesses to create joint content or organize events. This can lead to valuable inbound links, an important factor for SEO.

- **Leveraging social media:** Utilize social media platforms to promote your local content and interact with the community. This can increase direct traffic to your website and improve your online visibility.

MONITORING AND ADAPTATION

- **Performance analysis:** Use tools like Google Analytics and Google Search Console to monitor your website traffic, search rankings and user behavior, adjusting your strategy as needed.

- **Community feedback:** Keep an eye on local customer feedback and community trends to adapt your approach and content, keeping your brand relevant and engaging.

COMMON CHALLENGES

- **Visibility in competitive areas:** In highly competitive areas, standing out can be a challenge. Focus on specific niches and utilize unique stories and content to differentiate your brand.

- **Maintaining up-to-date information:** Your business information must remain consistent across all platforms and directories to avoid confusion and maximize local SEO.

As you enhance your local SEO strategy with these guerrilla tactics, the next chapter, "**ANALYSIS AND RAPID ADAPTATION**," will focus on how you can quickly measure success and adapt your digital marketing strategies to stay ahead of the competition. Are you ready to learn how to be agile and responsive in your marketing campaigns? Let's move forward, equipped with the tools to navigate and thrive in the dynamic local market.

# ANALYSIS AND RAPID ADAPTATION

In the fast-paced world of digital marketing, the ability to quickly analyze the performance of your campaigns and adapt your strategies can be the difference between success and failure. This chapter will explore how you can implement a continuous cycle of analysis and adaptation, ensuring your marketing tactics remain effective and relevant in the ever-changing digital landscape.

ESTABLISHING AN ANALYSIS SYSTEM

- **Define key metrics:** Identify which metrics are most important to your marketing goals. This can include conversion rates, engagement, website traffic, among others.

- **Use analytics tools:** Tools like Google Analytics, SEMrush and social media insights can provide valuable data on the performance of your campaigns.

- **Regular reporting:** Establish a schedule to review your metrics regularly. This could be daily, weekly or monthly depending on the nature of your campaigns.

INTERPRETING DATA FOR ADAPTATION

- **Identify trends:** Look for patterns or trends in the data that may indicate success or the need for adjustments in your campaigns.

- **A/B Testing:** Use A/B testing to try different approaches in your campaigns and determine what works best for your audience.

- **Listen to feedback:** Direct customer feedback, whether through comments, reviews or surveys, can provide valuable insights to improve your strategies.

ADAPTING QUICKLY

- **Be agile:** Prepare to make quick adjustments to your campaigns based on the data and feedback you collect. This might mean changing a message, adjusting a budget, or trying new distribution channels.

- **Constantly innovate:** The digital world is always evolving, so be open to trying new tactics or technologies to stay ahead.

- **Learn from mistakes:** See failures as learning opportunities. Analyze what didn't work and why to avoid repeating the same mistakes.

MAINTAINING RELEVANCE

- **Stay informed:** Stay on top of the latest market trends and platform updates to ensure your strategies remain relevant and effective.

- **Ongoing training:** Encourage ongoing training and development of your team to ensure they are equipped with the skills needed to implement effective digital marketing strategies.

With a robust system of analysis and rapid adaptation established, the next chapter, "**SMART AUTOMATION**", will explore how you can utilize technology to automate repetitive marketing tasks, allowing you to focus on creative strategies and data-driven decision making . Are you ready to optimize your processes and maximize the efficiency of your marketing campaigns? Let's move forward to discover the tools and techniques that will make a difference.

# SMART AUTOMATION

Intelligent automation in digital marketing is a powerful ally in process optimization, allowing marketing teams to save time on repetitive tasks and focus on high-value and creative strategies. This chapter covers how you can implement automation tools to improve the efficiency and effectiveness of your marketing campaigns, ensuring you are always one step ahead in your digital strategy.

BENEFITS OF AUTOMATION IN MARKETING

- **Operational efficiency:** Automate routine tasks such as social media posts, email marketing campaigns and audience segmentation to increase team productivity.

- **Personalization at scale:** Use customer data to automatically create personalized experiences, improving engagement and conversion.

- **Analysis and reporting:** Automated tools can collect and analyze large volumes of data, offering valuable insights with little manual effort.

IMPLEMENTING AUTOMATION

- **Identify tasks to automate:** Start with tasks that are time-consuming and easily standardizable, such as sending welcome emails, abandoned cart reminders, and publishing content on social media.

- **Choose the right tools:** Select automation tools that integrate well with the platforms you already use and that meet the specific needs of your business.

- **Define automatic workflows:** Create workflows that automatically perform tasks based on specific triggers, such as user actions or timing events.

BEST PRACTICES FOR SMART AUTOMATION

- **Maintain authenticity:** Make sure your automated

communication still reflects your brand voice and tone to maintain authenticity.

- **Continuous testing and optimization:** Monitor the performance of your automations regularly and make adjustments as needed to improve effectiveness.

- **Respect user privacy:** Use data responsibly, ensuring your automation complies with privacy regulations like GDPR.

RECOMMENDED AUTOMATION TOOLS

- **Email automation:** Tools like Mailchimp or Sendinblue for segmented and personalized email campaigns.

- **Social media management:** Platforms like Hootsuite or Buffer to schedule and publish content on various social networks.

- **CRM and marketing automation:** Systems like HubSpot or Salesforce to manage leads, customers and personalize the user journey.

Now that you understand the value of intelligent automation and how to implement it in your digital marketing strategies, the next chapter, " **LOW-COST LEAD GENERATION** ", will focus on innovative methods for capturing leads without large financial investments. Ready to explore creative and efficient lead generation techniques that can transform your sales funnel? Let's move on to discover how to maximize your conversion opportunities on a controlled budget.

# LOW-COST LEAD GENERATION

Lead generation is a crucial component of any digital marketing strategy, serving as the starting point for converting interested parties into loyal customers. However, many companies face the challenge of generating quality leads without exceeding budget limits. This chapter offers insights into how to maximize your lead generation opportunities using innovative, low-cost methods, ensuring your strategy is both effective and economically viable.

EFFECTIVE STRATEGIES FOR LOW-COST LEAD GENERATION

- **Valuable content:** Produce content that resonates with your target audience, such as e-books, infographics, webinars and blog posts. Content not only establishes your brand as an authority on the topic, but it can also be a powerful tool for capturing leads through signup forms.

- **SEO Optimization:** A strong online presence, optimized for search engines, can significantly increase your visibility and attract organic leads. Focus on relevant keywords, quality content, and a good website user experience.

- **Social media marketing:** Use social media platforms to engage with your audience and direct them to your website or registration landing pages. Creating communities or groups focused on specific topics can also be an excellent way to generate interested leads.

- **Strategic partnerships:** Collaborate with other companies or influencers who share a similar target audience. This could include content exchanges, joint webinars, or cross-promotional campaigns.

- **Segmented email campaigns:** Use email marketing to provide personalized and relevant content to different segments of your audience. Personalization can significantly increase open and conversion rates.

CREATIVE TACTICS FOR LEAD GENERATION

- **Contests and sweepstakes:** Organize contests or sweepstakes that encourage participation and sharing on social media. This can help expand your reach and capture contact information for interested attendees.

- **Engagement challenges:** Launch challenges that encourage interaction and content creation by users, using a specific hashtag to track participation and collect leads.

- **Referral marketing:** Encourage your current customers to refer friends or family in exchange for discounts or freebies. This method can generate high-quality leads at a relatively low cost.

## MONITORING SUCCESS AND ADJUSTING STRATEGIES

- **Data analysis:** Use analysis tools to monitor the performance of your lead generation strategies, identifying which tactics are producing the best results.

- **A/B Testing:** Try different calls to action, titles and layouts in your campaigns and landing pages to determine what generates the most leads.

- **Audience feedback:** Pay attention to feedback from your leads and customers to continually adjust and improve your fundraising strategies.

Mastering the art of low-cost lead generation puts your business in a strong position to grow and thrive in a competitive digital environment. The next chapter, " **GUERILLA ACTION PLAN** ", will consolidate everything we've learned, offering a step-by-step guide to implementing digital guerrilla tactics into your marketing strategy. Ready to put these ideas into action and boost the success of your business? Let's go ahead.

# GUERRILLA ACTION PLAN

After exploring a variety of digital guerrilla tactics, from strategic use of podcasts to low-cost lead generation, it's time to consolidate this knowledge into a tangible action plan. This final chapter will guide you in creating a detailed guerrilla action plan, enabling you to effectively apply the strategies discussed to achieve your marketing objectives with creativity, innovation, and cost effectiveness.

STEP 1: DEFINE YOUR MARKETING OBJECTIVES

The first step is to establish clear, measurable objectives for your guerrilla marketing campaign. Whether it's increasing brand awareness, generating leads, or driving sales, your goals should be Specific, Achievable, Relevant, and Time-Bound (SMART).

STEP 2: KNOW YOUR TARGET AUDIENCE

Develop a deep understanding of your target audience, including their wants, needs, behaviors and preferences. This will allow you to create campaigns that truly resonate with them and meet their expectations.

STEP 3: CHOOSE THE APPROPRIATE GUERRILLA TACTICS

Based on your goals and knowledge of your audience, select the digital guerrilla tactics that best fit your overall strategy. This can include any combination of the approaches discussed in previous chapters.

STEP 4: DEVELOP YOUR CONTENT

Create compelling, relevant content that supports your chosen tactics. This can range from blog posts and videos to interactive content and email campaigns. Remember to keep authenticity and creativity at the forefront.

STEP 5: RUN YOUR CAMPAIGN

With careful planning complete, it's time to launch your campaign. Be sure to closely monitor performance from the beginning, allowing you to make quick adjustments as needed.

## STEP 6: EVALUATE AND ADJUST

After launching the campaign, analyze its performance against the established objectives. Use the data collected to understand what worked well and what can be improved, adjusting your strategy for future campaigns.

## STEP 7: SCALABILITY AND REPETITION

Identify the most successful aspects of your campaign and consider how you can scale or repeat these tactics for even more success. Repetition, when done correctly, can solidify your brand presence and strengthen customer loyalty.

## MAINTAINING FLEXIBILITY

A key characteristic of guerrilla marketing is flexibility. Be prepared to adapt to changes in the market environment, emerging trends and public feedback. Maintaining an agile approach will allow you to maximize the impact of your digital guerrilla marketing campaigns.

## CONCLUSION

With this guerrilla action plan in hand, you are now equipped to implement creative, low-cost digital marketing strategies that can differentiate your brand in the competitive marketplace. Remember, the essence of guerrilla marketing lies in innovation and the ability to stand out from the crowd. By applying these principles, your brand will not only achieve its marketing goals but also create an authentic, lasting connection with your audience.

As we turn the final page of this journey together, I sincerely hope that the learnings shared here have touched your heart and sparked new perspectives. If this book has brought you any value, I kindly ask that you take a few moments to leave a review on Amazon. Your words not only help me grow and hone my craft, but they also guide other readers in their quests for knowledge and inspiration. Your opinion is a valuable gift, both for me and for the community of readers looking for stories that transform. I sincerely thank you for sharing this journey with me and I hope we can meet again in the pages of a new adventure.

# REGINALDO OSNILDO

Hello, I'm Reginaldo Osnildo, author and innovator in the fields of sales, technology, and communication strategies. My background spans from the academic setting, as a professor and researcher at the University of Southern Santa Catarina, to hands-on strategy development at the Catarinense Radio Group. With a PhD in sales narratives and digital convergence, and a Master's in storytelling and social imaginary, I offer my readers a unique blend of theory and practice. My aim is to deliver knowledge in a simple, practical, and didactic language, encouraging direct application in one's personal and professional life.

Yours sincerely

**Reginaldo Osnildo**

**+55 48 991913865**

**reginaldoosnildo@gmail.com**

www.ingramcontent.com/pod-product-compliance
Lightning Source LLC
Chambersburg PA
CBHW070343230526
45471CB00006B/2423